& BRIAN MILLS

A DIFFERENT COLLEGE EXPERIENCE

FOLLOWING CHRIST IN COLLEGE

Lifeway Students

EDITORIAL TEAM

Hamilton Barber
Writer

Kyle Wiltshire
Content Editor

Brooke Hill
Production Editor

Karen Daniel
Editorial Team Leader

John Paul Basham
Manager, Student Ministry Publishing

Ben Trueblood
Director, Student Ministry

Ross Funderburk
Art Direction

Published by Lifeway Press® • © 2022

No part of this work may be reproduced or transmitted in any form or by any means, electronic or mechanical, including photocopying and recording, or by any information storage or retrieval system, except as may be expressly permitted in writing by the publisher. Requests for permission should be addressed in writing to LifeWay Press®, One LifeWay Plaza, Nashville, TN 37234.

ISBN: 978-1-0877-4777-4

Item: 005833139

Dewey Decimal Classification Number: 248.83

Subject Heading: RELIGION/ CHRISTIAN MINISTRY/ YOUTH

Printed in the United States of America.

Student Ministry Publishing
Lifeway Resources
One Lifeway Plaza
Nashville, Tennessee 37234

We believe that the Bible has God for its author; salvation for its end; and truth, without any mixture of error, for its matter and that all Scripture is totally true and trustworthy. To review Lifeway's doctrinal guideline, please visit www.lifeway.com/doctrinalguideline.

Unless otherwise indicated, all Scripture quotations are taken from the Holy Bible, New Living Translation, copyright © 1996, 2004, 2007, 2013, 2015 by Tyndale House Foundation. Used by permission of Tyndale House Publishers, Inc., Carol Stream, IL 60188. All rights reserved.

TABLE OF CONTENTS

About the Authors	4
Introduction	5
How to Use this Study	6
Session 1: Identity	8
Session 2: The Church	20
Session 3: Relationships	32
Session 4: Wisdom	44
Leader Guide	56
Retreat Guide	62
Resources for Leaders	64
Resources for College Students	66
Resources for High School Seniors	68

ABOUT THE AUTHORS

Ben Trueblood serves as the Director of Student Ministry for Lifeway Christian Resources and has twenty years of student ministry experience, fourteen of which were spent in the local church as a student pastor. Ben is the author of three books, the host of The Student Ministry Podcast by Lifeway, is involved in training, consulting, and speaking to student ministries across the United States, and invests in youth pastors weekly through Student Ministry That Matters on YouTube. Ben and His wife Kristen have four children: Jonathan, Avery, Josiah, and Adrienne.

Brian Mills serves as the senior pastor of Trinity Baptist Church of Yukon, Oklahoma. Previously, he served as college pastor at Cross Church in Fayetteville, Arkansas, which reaches over 1,000 college students and young adults each week. He has authored three books and travels the country as a communicator of the gospel. He has led some of the largest student ministries in the country, along with serving as a teaching pastor since he began full-time ministry in 1999. Brian is happily married to Jennifer and they have two awesome children: McKenna and Parker.

INTRODUCTION

We wrote this study because we are passionate about high school and college students. Throughout our time in ministry, we've seen a lot of things go wrong in people's lives because of an incorrect view of the college experience. We want you to succeed in your college years and we believe that it can be the best experience of your life so far, but that will require you to make some difficult choices. You won't be able to approach your college experience like many of the people around you.

This study will help you understand more about your faith and help you to know how to make decisions that are built on the Word of God. When you are done with the next four (or more) years of your life, you should be more equipped than ever to embrace the life God has for you. We want to challenge you to take on that life with great wisdom and discernment.

During your college years, you will turn twenty-one, potentially find a spouse, be confronted with the greatest temptation you have ever faced, and have more freedom than you've ever known. Are you ready? The freshman-year mistakes happen because most are not. Don't let the college experience get the best of you; get the best of it. This study will help you do so.

—Ben and Brian

HOW TO USE THIS STUDY

A Different College Experience is a four-session Bible study designed to prepare and equip students for the college experience. It can be used as a companion resource to the 2019 book with the same name published by B&H Books, but it's not required to participate in this study.

The sessions are divided into three main sections—Getting Started, Study, and Next Steps. Each session includes a personal study and journaling pages for further reflection. A leader guide is also provided to prepare those who are walking students through this book in a group setting.

Getting Started provides questions that introduce the topic and helps generate discussion.

Study explores the session topic, shedding light on God's design for the college experience for students through exploration of His Word and thought-provoking questions.

Next Steps challenge students to apply what they've learned and continue the journey in their everyday lives.

Personal Study is intended to futher illustrate the session topic and help students as they navigate the college experience.

Journaling Pages are provided to answer questions from the personal study and for further reflection.

Leader Guide, found on pages 56-61 at the back of this book, helps you prepare each week. Use this guide to gain an understanding of the content for each session and learn ways to engage students in life-changing discussion.

Other Resources are found at the back of this book to facilitate this material in different environments and for unique audiences.

- **Retreat Guide** (pages 62-63) offers suggestions for how this material may be used in a retreat setting.
- **Resources for Leaders** (pages 64-65) gives leaders other resources they can use as they prepare students for and walk alongside them in their college experience.
- **Resources for College Students** (pages 66-67) guides current college students who want to walk through this study with friends.
- **Resources for High School Seniors** (pages 68-75) provides resources that will be helpful as students prepare for the college experience.

SESSION ONE

IDENTITY

GET STARTED

What is the most memorable trip you've ever taken?

What was it about that trip that stood out to you?

We've all been there: standing at the beginning of a journey. Our bags are packed. The car is gassed up. The plane tickets are bought. The stage is set, and what lies ahead is a voyage into the unknown. Just the open road or open sky, and a journey and a destination before us.

The Christian life is not much different, but on a much bigger scale. It's the journey of an entire life, the destination—eternity. Right now, you are already somewhere on this journey: some of you have only just begun; others have been on the way for years. Regardless of where you find yourself, let's start at the beginning so that we can run—and finish—our journeys well.

STUDY

At the beginning of every Christian's journey, and at the center of our very lives, is the gospel: the good news about Jesus.

In your own words, what do you think the gospel is?

How have you seen the gospel affect your life?

READ GENESIS 1:1 AND REVELATION 4:11.

> *In the beginning God created the heavens and the earth.*
>
> *Our Lord and God,*
> *you are worthy to receive*
> *glory and honor and power,*
> *because you have created all things,*
> *and by your will*
> *they exist and were created.*

Why do you think we should start talking about the gospel by talking about God?

Any gospel presentation or discussion that doesn't start with God doesn't start at the beginning. The gospel is not about us, it's about our Creator, His faithfulness, and His provision for us even though we are unworthy. He is perfect and holy. The gospel is His work in our lives, not something that we do to earn His favor.

We were created in God's image, but, as we move through what the gospel is, we learn that we veered away from Him.

READ JEREMIAH 17:9 AND ROMANS 3:23.

> *The heart is more deceitful than anything else, and incurable—who can understand it?*
>
> *For all have sinned and fall short of the glory of God.*

What do you think the difference is between being a "good person" and being a sinner?

How can we say that "all have sinned"? What does it mean to be a sinner?

You've probably heard something like this before: "I'm not perfect, but I'm not all bad." Scripture tells us the opposite. There is nobody who is righteous on their own (see Rom. 3:10-12).

What's more, Jesus consistently raised the bar for holiness: "not all bad" isn't good enough. For example, in His Sermon on the Mount, Jesus said that it isn't good enough not to commit murder; you must also not be angry with your brother or sister (see Matt. 5:21-22). The problem at the root of this isn't that we're just not good enough, it's that our hearts are sick. The best that we can do on our own looks like dirty rags in God's eyes (see Isa. 64:6).

READ 2 CORINTHIANS 5:20-21.

> *Therefore, we are ambassadors for Christ, since God is making his appeal through us. We plead on Christ's behalf, "Be reconciled to God." He made the one who did not know sin to be sin for us, so that in him we might become the righteousness of God.*

Why is the resurrection of Jesus so crucial to the gospel?

How would you explain Jesus's sacrifice on the cross to someone who has never heard of it before?

If Jesus didn't rise from the dead, He wasn't who He said He was, the penalty we owe for our sin hasn't been paid, and, quite frankly, we live in hopelessness.

Fortunately for us, Jesus is who He said He is. He *did* rise from the dead. He *did* conquer sin and death on the cross. He rose from the grave, doing exactly what He said He would do, proving Himself to be the only Savior we can put our faith in.

Amazingly, when we see ourselves through the light of the gospel, it not only changes the way we see ourselves, it changes the way we see God.

What comes into your mind when you think about God?

To some, God is a piece of a puzzle that you drop into place when you can't find anything else to put there. He's a unknowable sky-genie, or just a comforting thought in troubling times.

When God is just another puzzle piece in your life, you're putting Him somewhere He doesn't belong. You are trying to cram Him into a box you've made for Him. God is not a piece of the puzzle; He is the entire frame. He is the lens through which you see everything and everyone. He is the one who makes the other pieces fit; He isn't what you plug in to an otherwise incomplete picture.

Seeing God for who He truly is will take your breath away. Below, there are some Scripture references. Read each and then write a sentence describing what you learn about God through them:

Isaiah 6:1-8

Ephesians 2:1-10

Genesis 1

Job 38

Seeing God for who He is doesn't only change the way we see God, it changes the way we view ourselves.

We're surrounded by people telling us who we're supposed to be. They may tell us we have to have a social media following or develop a personal brand. They may tell us we have to acquire new tech or dress in a certain way. Because of these voices, you may feel like your identity is tied to what you can produce.

All of that is a lie. And when we view ourselves in light of the gospel, we take steps toward believing the truth about ourselves: that we are sinners saved by the grace of our Creator.

What is the difference between the way the world sees us and the way God does?

How does that affect the way you go about your everyday life?

READ COLOSSIANS 2:13-14.

> *And when you were dead in trespasses and in the uncircumcision of your flesh, he made you alive with him and forgave us all our trespasses. He erased the certificate of debt, with its obligations, that was against us and opposed to us, and has taken it away by nailing it to the cross.*

How does the gospel change the way you see yourself?

How does this new view of yourself motivate you to live?

If you are a child of God, you are *forgiven*. You have been made clean. Whenever God looks at you, He doesn't see the one who was dead (see Eph. 2), He sees someone who has been made clean by Jesus's sacrifice. Your sin has been nailed to the cross and He has removed the guilt and shame that goes along with it.

For those of us who have been made new by Jesus, we can rest in the truth that we are valuable because we're created in His image, we're loved because God loved us first, and we have been made clean by Jesus's sacrifice—it was nothing that we did. We have been given everything we need through Jesus to live out this new life right now.

This reality is not just an interesting fact about us; it's everything about who we are. This truth guides us, and it's crucial to us getting the college experience right.

NEXT STEPS

Living out the holiness we've been called to and given by Jesus is not something we'll know how to do overnight. Becoming the person Jesus is making us into is a lifelong process called sanctification. Sanctification is growth: growth into the kind of life that Jesus calls us to live. And God has given us all the tools we need to continually grow in sanctification.

What are some steps that you can take to grow into someone like Jesus?

What are some practical ways you can live out the gospel in your everyday life?

PERSONAL STUDY

Have you ever seen a big word used to describe something that is fairly simple?

Here's a fun one to throw around at parties: **defenestration**. It sounds fancy because it has five syllables full of consonants, but it means something far simpler than it may seem:

Throwing something out of a window.

Words are funny like that. It's tricky to capture the essence of an idea in a single word, but that doesn't stop us from trying. The same thing happens with a word that is going to carry us through this study: **sanctification**.

Simply put, sanctification is just growing in obedience to God. But even this definition doesn't perfectly capture it.

Read the following explanation of what sanctification is. Note the graph to help you picture what sanctification looks like in your life.

Sanctification: Growing in Obedience

> *The process of learning to obey God and growing in our obedience is something the Bible refers to as "sanctification." There are two sides to this word. The first side is something that happens the moment a person first believes in Jesus. Because of Jesus's perfect life, sacrifice, and resurrection, God declares us not guilty of our sin (also know as justification) and at the same time He also declares us perfect and holy. God sees you as holy because He sees you through His Son. Right now, in terms of standing before God, you as a believer in Jesus are as holy as you will ever be. It's so important to let that truth sink in because it changes everything about the way you approach growing in obedience to God. You don't obey God to acquire more holiness. You don't obey God to make Him happy or to keep Him from being angry with you. He already sees you as holy because of Jesus. Obedience to God has nothing to do with us earning anything; it's all been earned for us by Jesus. This means that the Christian life is not about waking up every day and trying harder or willing yourself to obey God, but instead learning to live out who God has already said you are through Jesus. While the first side of sanctification isn't something you participate in, you do participate in the second side. The sanctification that you experience in this life is the actual process of growing in your obedience to God. It is the process you are on to become more like Jesus, to become more holy throughout your lifetime. Here's what that process looks like visually:*[1]

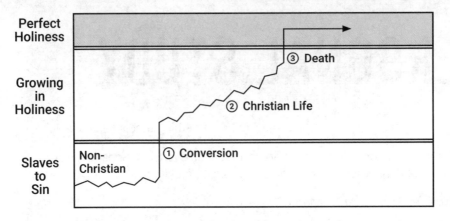

The Process of Sanctification

> *Nathan Bingham from Ligonier Ministries says it this way: "Sanctification is growth. In regeneration [when you first believe in Jesus], God implants desires that were not there before: desire for God, for holiness, and for glorifying God's name in the world; desire to pray and worship; desire to love and bring benefit to others."[2] These are desires that we don't create or conjure up; they are given to us, "implanted" within us as a gift from God at salvation. As these desires grow, so will your obedience to God, and God has provided the way for these desires to continue growing in you.*

On your own, journal through the questions below. You can use the Journaling Pages on 17-19 of this book. Then, this week, meet up with someone who is currently going through this study with you to talk about your answers:

What stuck out to you while you were reading?

Where do you think you are on the graph? Why?

What are some practical ways to grow in sanctification?

JOURNALING PAGES

SESSION TWO

THE CHURCH

GET STARTED

It's rare that we get to see the beginning of something that absolutely takes off—whether it's a meme, a fashion trend, an event, or a movement. Imagine being one of the first subscribers of your favorite Youtuber or being at an early gig of a now famous band that you love. These things typically start with just a few people before becoming something that millions of people hear about, love, and follow.

But we're all sitting exactly where we are doing exactly what we're doing for a reason, and what's most interesting about that is we were around to see the beginning steps: the things that brought us to where we are now.

Think about something cool that you're involved in right now. It might be an activity, a field you're studying, or an opportunity that has come your way. What are some of the things in your life that led you to this place?

We don't usually think about it this way, but one of the oldest movements that people still take part in is Jesus's church. Let's take a few minutes to talk about what the church is and why it's so incredible and important to take part in to make the most of your college experience.

STUDY

If you had to describe "church" in one or two sentences, what would you say?

For all practical purposes, the church is just a bunch of people who are all devoted to the same idea: that Jesus is the Son of God, that He is risen, and that these truths motivate us to live in a certain way.

That's actually exactly how it started. After Jesus's resurrection, one of His disciples, Peter, got up and preached a sermon in the middle of Jerusalem, and before he and the other hundred or so believers knew it, *three thousand people* were added to their number.

Look at how they dealt with this:

READ ACTS 2:42-47.

> They devoted themselves to the apostles' teaching, to the fellowship, to the breaking of bread, and to prayer.
>
> Everyone was filled with awe, and many wonders and signs were being performed through the apostles. Now all the believers were together and held all things in common. They sold their possessions and property and distributed the proceeds to all, as any had need. Every day they devoted themselves to meeting together in the temple, and broke bread from house to house. They ate their food with joyful and sincere hearts, praising God and enjoying the favor of all the people. Every day the Lord added to their number those who were being saved.

Look at some of the things the early church was involved in. What do you notice about it?

What do you think was attractive about the community described in this passage?

What about it would have made you want to join them?

The amazing thing about the church at this point was that it was wildly unstructured, yet it perfectly fit the needs of the people it reached. They didn't even have their own building! Jerusalem had a temple, of course, but that place was not where this movement found its footing: the power of the early church was in the people who had received *their* power from the Holy Spirit.

When the Spirit entered these people, the result was radical hospitality. They looked out for each other. They shared meals together. They dove into the apostles' teaching together. They were all in—not just for the people around them, but for the gospel that united them.

And get this: it filled everyone with awe. Even those not in the church.

Why do you think that the actions and attitudes of the people in the early church filled those around them with awe?

Think about your local church for a second. Where do you see these same actions and attitudes today?

The Greek word used for "community" in this passage is *koinonia*. When people share *koinonia*, it means something different than just being in close proximity to each other. It means that they are united by a common goal—in this case, the gospel of Jesus. Because of what united them, it didn't matter what they looked like or where they came from. They had the most powerful unifying factor right at their center—the gospel.

The church was birthed out of our need for one another, both physically and spiritually. When we have a community around us who is committed to Jesus, we are continuing what began two thousand years ago.

The author of Hebrews had specific instructions to people in these early church communities around the world:

READ HEBREWS 10:24-25.

> *And let us consider one another in order to provoke love and good works, not neglecting to gather together, as some are in the habit of doing, but encouraging each other, and all the more as you see the day approaching.*

Consider what we read in Acts 2 along with this passage. Why is it so important for believers to meet together?

What do you miss out on by not being involved with a local body of believers?

Whenever we see the church mentioned in Scripture, it actually goes a lot deeper than just acknowledging it as a group of people united with a common goal. It serves a function much bigger than that: it is called the **body of Christ**. Since Jesus is not physically present among us, we are called His body. When the world wants to see what Jesus looks like, they should look no further than the church.

READ 1 CORINTHIANS 12:12-14.

> *For just as the body is one and has many parts, and all the parts of that body, though many, are one body—so also is Christ. For we were all baptized by one Spirit into one body—whether Jews or Greeks, whether slaves or free—and we were all given one Spirit to drink. Indeed, the body is not one part but many.*

Why do you think a "body" is an appropriate metaphor for what the church is?

How does seeing the church as a "body" affect the way you see individual members of it?

Since the church is the physical representation of Christ to the world, that means each member has incredible individual worth. When a body is perfectly functioning, each of its organs, systems, and limbs are working together with the rest of the body to achieve the overall goal of health and productivity.

The church is not going to be full of productive members if the members are isolated and operating all on their own accord. We must learn to work together in humility if we're going to be the healthy body of Christ.

Read what Peter had to say about this:

READ 1 PETER 5:5.

> *In the same way, you who are younger, be subject to the elders. All of you clothe yourselves with humility toward one another, because God resists the proud but gives grace to the humble.*

Why is it is important to respect and have relationships with older, more seasoned members of the body of Christ?

What is a way you've been grown in your process of sanctification by learning from generations who came before you?

One of the simplest ways to ensure you are working as a productive member of Christ's body is to learn from those who've been where you are before. Being plugged into a local, healthy body of Christ is absolutely essential for anybody living out their faith in Jesus and pursuing sanctification. A local church will help you when you are in physical need, will help you grow in your faith, and will speak wisdom into your life from a place of experience and patience.

The church, like a body, doesn't function best when all of its individual parts are not present, available, and fulfilling their role. You have a role in the body in your college years. To get the most from your college experience, make the local church a vital part of your life. A local church will bless you, sustain you, encouarge you, and support you during this crucial time in your spiritual development.

NEXT STEPS

This week, consider some of the older members of your local church congregation—those who have seen the seasons change and stayed faithful through them all. If you already have a relationship with one, reach out and ask to just sit with them for a little while. Talk to them about some of what we learned in this session. Ask them questions and listen to how they answer. Consider questions such as:

- **How did you come to faith in Christ?**
- **How did you cultivate your faith during your college years?**
- **What are habits you keep that help you grow in your relationship with God?**
- **What has been a difficult time you've walked through in your life? How did your relationship with God sustain you through it?**
- **How has the local church helped you grow in your relationshp with God? Others?**

If you don't already have a relationship with an older person from your church, reach out to your pastor and ask for an introduction to someone you can learn and grow from. You'll undoubtedly find that a visit or even a phone call will be received with open arms and you will be all the more healthy for it.

All of these first "Next Steps" assume you are involved in a local church. The reality is, you may not have a local church you faithfully attend yet. If you don't, take these next steps:

- **Pray that God would direct you to a place where you can serve and be served.**
- **Don't look for the perfect church—it doesn't exist. If you don't know where to begin, start with the church closest to where you live and go from there.**
- **Don't make excuses. Set an alarm clock (or three) and get to church on the next Sunday morning. Attend worship and a small group you can potentially connect with.**
- **Don't be discouraged if it takes some time to find the right fit. Don't give up! The Holy Spirit will direct you to the right place where you can plug in.**

PERSONAL STUDY

If you're not there already, you're about to learn something that will remain true for the rest of your life:

You are busy.

Think about all the things that demand your time and attention: your course load, extracurricular activities, job, study time, relationships, etc. This doesn't even factor in any time to eat and sleep. It won't be long (if it isn't already) until your go-to answer when people ask how you've been will be "busy."

Life gets *busy*. But this is nothing new. Think about Jesus's life: repeatedly throughout His ministry, He was surrounded by crowds of people clamoring to hear Him speak, asking Him to heal them, and trying to trap Him with trick questions. His schedule was so packed that each of the gospel writers takes time to specifically describe momnents when He had to retreat to be by Himself and spend time with God.

Busyness is nothing new. Still, the author of Hebrews tells us that, even in the day it was written, it was crucial for believers to not stop meeting together (see Heb. 10:25). This is because people were built for community. We stand alongside one another to help each other with our burdens—whether it's personal struggles or simply a busy schedule.

Read the story of Joe Massey, who made time for community despite having a busy schedule. See where you find similarities between his life and yours.

> *I began serving in my church at the beginning of my junior year, and it was by accident. My schedule at that time was very busy and so I had very few breaks, but I would always be sure to take a break to attend my church's Wednesday night college service. I had a very small window of time to get dinner after class on Wednesdays, so I would have to get food and then take it to the church and eat it outside before going in for the service. Every time I would arrive, people would joke around and laugh because I was eating dinner on the sidewalk, but I began to get to know the other students who served the church because they'd always talk to me. As we talked, I would help them out by setting up tables or extra chairs and just doing anything that I was asked to do. As I continued to serve each week, I began to realize how much joy serving my fellow students brought me and how it laid a foundation for me to form relationships with everyone that came through the doors.*
>
> *I was then given more responsibility by our pastor and the other leaders in our church, which increased my area of influence while also encouraging me to serve more. Throughout all of this time, my schedule was still just as busy as before—I was the vice president of my fraternity, I was studying or doing homework every night, and I was leading a weekly Bible study group. I learned that even though I wasn't required to*

serve the church every week, it was a time that God would reveal biblical truths to me. Even though it seemed like I could've taken those extra hours to catch up on sleep or homework, I knew that the Lord was going to use me in some way.

Mark 10:43–45 says, "But it is not so among you. On the contrary, whoever wants to become great among you will be your servant, and whoever wants to be first among you will be a slave to all. For even the Son of Man did not come to be served, but to serve, and to give his life as a ransom for many." In this passage, Jesus was telling His disciples about the importance of serving others, and if they put the needs of others before their own, they would be made great. In the same way, the Lord has taught me so many things through time spent serving the church and He has strengthened me in multiple areas of my life.

—Joe Massey, vice president of Beta Upsilon Chi at the University of Arkansas; senior medical student

Journal through the questions below. When you meet up with the person you planned in this week's Next Step, ask them the same questions and see how they compare.

When do you think the busiest time of your life was?

What role does community play in your life?

When have others helped you through something you've been struggling with?

JOURNALING PAGES

SESSION THREE

RELATIONSHIPS

GET STARTED

Who is the person you know best in the world? Describe them.

Who do you think knows you best? How do you know?

One of the purest joys we can experience in life is that of being *known*. When we can be ourselves around someone else and know that we can trust them, and that they can trust us, we experience the kind of beauty that comes from true, authentic relationships with the people around us. College is a time when many people form the deepest relationships they'll have in their lives.

As Christians, we're called to a high standard when it comes to those around us. We won't know everyone we encounter as deeply as those who are closest to us, but God has made the standard for treating those around us unmistakably clear. As we learn to treat them the way we've been commanded to, we'll learn about ourselves, other people, and God.

STUDY

As we continue to grow in the Lord and learn to walk in righteousness, we will be constantly on the lookout for the ways He is molding us into His image. Part of what that looks like is living the way He told us to.

READ LUKE 10:25-28.

> *Then an expert in the law stood up to test him, saying, "Teacher, what must I do to inherit eternal life?"*

> "What is written in the law?" he asked him. "How do you read it?"
>
> He answered, "Love the Lord your God with all your heart, with all your soul, with all your strength, and with all your mind," and "your neighbor as yourself."
>
> "You've answered correctly," he told him. "Do this and you will live."

In your own words, what makes what is written in verse 27 the "greatest commandment"?

What kinds of actions show that you love the Lord?

What kinds of actions show that you love your neighbor as yourself?

Matthew 22:35-40 tells us that when Jesus was asked what the greatest commandment was, He answered with exactly what this expert in the law said in verse 27. This commandment is actually two separate ones, but they flow together perfectly: if you love God with everything that you are, that love will naturally flow out to the people around you.

The reason is simple: if we love God, we will love those who bear God's image the same way. Genesis 1:26-27 shows us that every person ever created, no matter who they are, was created by God with the incredibly important distinction of being made in His image with characteristics that resemble Him and which point to Him as their Creator. We cannot claim to love God if we do not love the people around us.

READ 1 CORINTHIANS 13:1-3.

> If I speak human or angelic tongues but do not have love, I am a noisy gong or a clanging cymbal. If I have the gift of prophecy and understand all mysteries and all knowledge, and if I have all faith so that I can move mountains but do not have love, I am nothing. And if I give away all my possessions, and if I give over my body in order to boast but do not have love, I gain nothing.

In your own words, what is love?

The ancient Greeks had four different words for love, each of which has its own meaning:

Agape: unconditional love, like God's love for us.

Philia: brotherly love, like love between friends.

Eros: romantic love, like love between spouses.

Storge: familial love, like love from a parent to a child or between siblings.

What do each of these kinds of love have in common?

How can you tell if someone is treating you with love?

Not everyone is going to be able to communicate with you in the specific way that you receive love best, but you can always tell if someone is treating you with love if they are showing you selflessness and respect. This is how Paul can say that it doesn't matter what good we accomplish or what feats we can manage if we don't have love. If we can't show our neighbor love—no matter who they are—how can we say that we love the Creator who made them?

READ MATTHEW 5:43-48.

> "You have heard that it was said, Love your neighbor and hate your enemy. But I tell you, love your enemies and pray for those who persecute you, so that you may be children of your Father in heaven. For he causes his sun to rise on the evil and the good, and sends rain on the righteous and the unrighteous. For if you love those who love you, what reward will you have? Don't even the tax collectors do the same? And if you greet only your brothers and sisters, what are you doing out of the ordinary? Don't even the Gentiles do the same? Be perfect, therefore, as your heavenly Father is perfect."

SESSION THREE: RELATIONSHIPS

In this passage, Jesus laid out the standard for how we are to treat even our greatest enemies in no uncertain terms. These can be difficult words to read because it is *not* easy to love other people, especially if they've wronged us. But Jesus made no distinctions or exceptions.

What are some of the excuses we come up with to explain why someone in our lives isn't worth loving?

How have you seen people justify acting poorly to one another?

Have you ever been shown selfless love like the kind of love Jesus described in this passage? How?

You are going into some of the most crucial years of your life. You are going to be surrounded by people you weren't around growing up, who believe all sorts of things about the ways that people are supposed to treat each other.

That is okay. Christians are very familiar with living in this tension between what the world expects and what Jesus has called them to. The kind of love we are to show those around us is not something that has an earthly origin: it comes from God, who loved us first in the same way.

How can the way you treat those around you communicate the gospel without even saying a word?

What are some ways that you see brokenness in the relationships around you?

How do Jesus's words in Matthew 5:43-48 address that brokenness?

One of the most evident places you will see relational brokenness in college is when it comes to sex. Applying these Scriptural principles to our understanding of sex can revolutionize your college experience. They will help you as you date and seek out a potential spouse. They will assist you with the dangers of pornography and guide your heart when tempted toward premarital sex.

The gospel has the power to address the brokenness that can come from sex apart from God's design and unhealthy relationships. When we begin from the understanding that every single person is created in God's image, that every single person is a sinner like us, and that there isn't a single person who has ever lived or who will ever live who is exempt from Jesus's sacrifice, we are able to live in relationship with others in a more productive and God-honoring way.

College is a wonderful time for relationships, but it can also be destructive. Keeping this foundational view of love at the forefront of your mind and heart and applying it to all your relationships can keep you from decisions that can negatively alter your life and can help foritfy friendships that will last a lifetime.

NEXT STEPS

Treating other people as though they, too, were made in the image of God is difficult. But it is an important step in our sanctification—our growing in Christlikeness. It comes through practice, but it also comes through the help of the Holy Spirit.

Take a little bit of time to address some of the brokenness you see in relationships around you. Begin with the understanding that each person involved has been hand-crafted in the image of God, and then work from there to discover how best to love them.

Who is somebody in your life you can show selfless, God-honoring love to this week?

What is a plan you can put in place to make sure you see this through?

PERSONAL STUDY

It's time to address the elephant in the room. You're reading a book about a different kind of college experience. You've just had a discussion about relationships. You are entering, or already in, your twenties. What is the first thing that comes to your mind when you hear "relationships"?

Scripture has a *lot* to say about the relationships you're thinking of: your relationship with the person you are dating. The person you want to date. The person you will marry. Humans are built with this thinking in mind.

Be honest with yourself: what are your expectations when it comes to romantic love? In the next few years, you're going to have opportunities like you haven't had before. New freedoms. New temptations.

But listen to this: the basis for our romantic relationships is the same as our relationships with those around us. They begin by seeing the other person not as an opportunity to get something from them, but by seeing them as they truly are: people made in the image of God for whom the King of kings gave His life.

Read the story of John and Ellie Wilson:.

> *We met during a time in our lives that neither of us would say we were looking for a spouse, or even looking to date. It was completely God's timing. For the first month of knowing each other, we were in two different states and communicated through texting and phone calls. That first month was vital to our relationship because we began to peel back layers and really get to know each other. This created a foundation of friendship for our future relationship. Once we started dating, our friendship and communication continued growing and we began to develop trust.*
>
> *Our relationship was, and still is, a sanctification process. Neither of us had been in a godly relationship before, but we both knew that's what we wanted. In the beginning, honestly, it wasn't perfect. We were figuring out how we could honor God through a dating relationship, and along the way had to make changes in our personal habits and habits as a couple. Our intentions were pure, and God showed us so much grace while gently gifting us with wisdom, conviction, and courage to strengthen our relationship. Although in the beginning we felt clueless as how to have a "godly relationship," we were open with one another and willing to hand selfish desires of the flesh over to God.*
>
> *Boundaries were something it felt as if we were always trying to understand. The harder we tried to discern what "good boundaries" were, the more apparent they became. The Bible makes it clear that there should not even be a hint of sexual immorality, which basically means that any form of sexuality needs to be saved for marriage. When trying to live that out for the first time, it is easy to think that God is completely against sex and wonder why He would want to keep these pleasurable things from us. Through prayer*

and conversation with God, it becomes evident that the Lord gives these guidelines for our protection. The scars caused by sexual sin are some of the deepest scars, and if we're being honest, most people have them. This understanding reveals that the Lord does not give us this direction with the intention of depriving us from something great, but rather to protect us and then bless us in the security of marriage.

In our dating relationship, we knew we could trust each other because there was a deep conviction in both of us anytime we crossed a boundary. We openly talked about it with one another and repented before God. We have learned that it's just as important to ask God to give you courage to change your course of action when feeling convicted as it is to pray that God will convict you. Whenever we acted out of the will of God, we would feel convicted, but it was our conviction in action that was so important to the course of our relationship. After falling into sin, it is vital to have boldness to openly talk about your feelings of conviction and work with your boyfriend/girlfriend in how you can move forward from there.

One thing that was a good sign early in our relationship was that the majority of our conversations centered around the Lord. We talked about our personal God-given passions, things of this world that hurt our heart, and stories of redemption in our lives. As we began to understand each other's hearts more, we began to encourage and challenge one another to take steps of faith to advance God's kingdom. We prayed for one another and God gave us a heart to love each other more. All of this was out of the overflow of our individual love and passion for Jesus Christ.

A major key in our relationship was the community that we had surrounding us. We attended a college small group where we were welcomed and unjudged by fellow Christians. The friends that we made through that community walked with us through times of joy, times of conflict, and times of hurt. Specifically, one couple in the group poured wisdom and counsel into us while inviting us into their lives where we could observe how they glorified the Lord through their relationship. This community and these friendships were extremely important in the health of our own relationship. By no means is our relationship perfect, but the Lord continues to grow us in Him and with each other.

—*John and Ellie Wilson*

Journal your thoughts and answers to the questions below and reach out to the person you meet up with on the first week to talk about some of them.

What are your personal boundaries in romantic relationships? Where do they come from?

How can you use your community to encourage you in your convictions?

What role has prayer played in your relationships in the past? In your relationship now? How would you like to see that change?

JOURNALING PAGES

SESSION FOUR

WISDOM

GET STARTED

Imagine you're experiencing a problem you've never seen before. Maybe your car is making a noise you've never heard or the faucet in your dorm room has sprung a leak.

When facing a new problem, which of these do you tend to do first: try to handle the problem yourself or reach out to someone who knows how to do it better?

When you have tried to handle the problem yourself, what has been the result?

When you have reached out to someone else who knows how to do it better, what has been the result?

Some people tend to be do-it-yourselfers. These people are probably hesitant to reach out and ask for help, at least until they've exhausted everything for themselves. The others aren't hesitant to reach out for help at all: they understand that someone else might know how to fix the issue better than they do.

Eventually, you're going to come across situations that aren't solved with a simple internet search or YouTube video. You need wisdom. Wisdom can be quite a bit trickier than we tend to give it credit for. During your college years, very little will be more useful to avoid pitfalls and for your experience than finding wisdom.

STUDY

READ JAMES 1:5-8.

> *Now if any of you lacks wisdom, he should ask God—who gives to all generously and ungrudgingly—and it will be given to him. But let him ask in faith without doubting. For the doubter is like the surging sea, driven and tossed by the wind. That person should not expect to receive anything from the Lord, being double-minded and unstable in all his ways.*

In your own words, what do you think wisdom is?

How is it different than knowledge?

What places do people generally turn to when looking for wisdom?

Wisdom is the ability to decide right from wrong, whether that means discerning the right attitude to have or the right action to take. There are thousands of places we tend to turn when looking for wisdom, ranging from persuasive people who have written books and developed programs, to people with large followings on social media, and even sometimes simply "trusting our gut." James pointed out that we can bypass any human-centered source of wisdom and focus on the One who gives it to any who ask Him for it.

Look back at James 1:5. What does it tell you about God's character?

How have you experienced God's generosity toward you?

The more we experience God, the more we find that generosity is one of His most apparent qualities and His mercy is unending. If we are living as His children and we ask Him for wisdom, of course He will give it to us. He is our Shepherd, and His wisdom is one of the tools He gives to safeguard us from walking into pitfalls and things that can cause us harm.

Going into this season of your life, you will be facing new situations and decisions you may not have experienced yet where you have to depend on wise decision-making. Let's look at a few of those situations now, but through the lens of Solomon, who provided some scenarios where the Lord's wisdom really comes in handy.

READ PROVERBS 2:12-18.

> [Wisdom] will rescue you from the way of evil—
> from anyone who says perverse things,
> from those who abandon the right paths
> to walk in ways of darkness,
> from those who enjoy doing evil
> and celebrate perversion,
> whose paths are crooked,
> and whose ways are devious.
> It will rescue you from a forbidden woman,
> from a wayward woman with her flattering talk,
> who abandons the companion of her youth
> and forgets the covenant of her God;
> for her house sinks down to death
> and her ways to the land of the departed spirits.

These words are thousands of years old, but still they feel fresh and relevant to us today. How do you see some of these situations still today?

Where do you think God's wisdom and the world's wisdom might contradict each other?

You might find some of these situations hitting a little close to home. That's because people haven't fundamentally changed all that much over the years. We still struggle with the same things, there are just many new ways to do the same old things today.

What's more, the way God teaches us to deal with them doesn't always look like the way the world does. James warned his audience against being "double-minded," which refers to someone who is driven and tossed constantly by the changing wind of worldly wisdom.

If you are going into this next season of your life relying on worldly wisdom, odds are you are going to end up pretty frustrated. You can find all sorts of worldly philosophies to justify any number of actions you could ever take. But these next few years could be an incredible opportunity to do something that will set a foundation under your feet for years to come: to *grow* in godly wisdom.

READ PROVERBS 3:5-12.

> Trust in the Lord with all your heart,
> and do not rely on your own understanding;
> in all your ways know him,
> and he will make your paths straight.
> Don't be wise in your own eyes;
> fear the Lord and turn away from evil.
> This will be healing for your body
> and strengthening for your bones.
> Honor the Lord with your possessions
> and with the first produce of your entire harvest;
> then your barns will be completely filled,
> and your vats will overflow with new wine.
> Do not despise the Lord's instruction, my son,
> and do not loathe his discipline;
> for the Lord disciplines the one he loves,
> just as a father disciplines the son in whom he delights.

Proverbs 9:10 tells us that the fear of the Lord is the beginning of wisdom. One of the ways we develop a healthy fear, or reverent respect, for the Lord is through growing in our trust of Him.

Reflect on a time when you trusted someone, only to have that trust broken.

What does it take for you to put your trust in somebody?

The unfortunate truth is that each of you probably has a story about putting your trust in somebody else and being let down by them. This is not to say we shouldn't learn to trust the people around us; rather, it should highlight how exceptional it is to trust the Lord. Never in all of history has the Lord broken even an ounce of trust that somebody has put in Him.

This passage shows us some tangible ways we can learn to put our trust in God, primarily through our possessions. If we can learn to trust God with the things that we have, we will soon learn how to translate that trust into intangible things like decisions and desires and direction for our lives.

What do you think it looks like to honor God with your possessions?

How would that affect the things that you want?

For many people, honoring God with what they have is the first step toward developing a growing and mature trust in His wisdom. It's just the beginning of a lifelong relationship where the Lord speaks into your decision-making—whether it is where you put your money or how you approach a difficult crossroads.

And what is most remarkable about all of this is that as you put more and more trust in Him, He will never, ever let you down. The college experience is just plain better when it's not littered with bad decision after bad decision. The way to avoid bad decisions is to lean on the wisdom that comes from God.

NEXT STEPS

In the coming years, you are going to be faced with situations where acting wisely is more crucial than ever. But learning to live a life of God-honoring wisdom is not just something that will serve you well in college, it will carry you through the rest of your life.

Take a few minutes on your own to re-read Proverbs 2:12-18. In the space below, jot down some real-life scenarios that correspond to each of the situations it presents, and then write down a godly response to each of them.

Scripture: **Real-life Scenario:**   **Godly Response:**

PERSONAL STUDY

There was a boy born in South Africa in the early 70s who was so frequently silent and lost in his own head that his parents actually had his hearing tested. It turns out, his hearing was fine; he was just completely lost in his thoughts.

This continued through his childhood and took off when he turned ten and got his hands on a computer. He started learning to code and, two years later, sold his first piece of software: a game which he called Blastar.

He honed his skills religiously over the next ten years and, when he turned twenty-four, he and his brother launched a company which sold a few years later for $307 million. He used his portion of the money to launch a website that turned into Paypal—a service that we still use to this day. He later went on to found his third company, SpaceX. His name is Elon Musk.[3]

Though Elon Musk can be a bit of a touchy subject, he is one of thousands of examples of what discipline looks like. Instead of focusing on frivolous things, he looked only at his goal.

As you learn to grow in Godliness—as you are *sanctified*—you'll need this same kind of focus. With eyes trained on Jesus, it gets harder to become distracted by things that simply do not matter. It will change the way you see yourself, those around you, and decisions that you are faced with.

Turn your attention to Zach Morris's personal account.

> *My story with God starts out like the majority of others who call the Bible Belt home. I've heard all God has to say in His Word since day one. I heard the gospel and experienced salvation by grace through faith in Jesus alone at a young age. When I became a teenager, though, I started listening to something different. Peer pressure. Lust. Pride. I remember thinking to myself, I'm young, so I can live how I want to live now and come back to this Jesus lifestyle later. What a bad thought that led to even worse choices of pornography, pride in my athletics, and other sinful postures.*
>
> *That's when God taught me to be wise the hard way. When I was fifteen and not walking with Jesus, our church got a new youth pastor, Randy Presley. Honestly, I didn't like the guy at first, but God used him in an incredible way to bring me back to God. He left the ninety-nine sheep to go after the one—me. Randy and I started getting closer as the year went on. He started teaching me all that it meant to live my life with faith in Jesus. I came to a moment after my first mission trip to Zambia where the Lord took me to my knees in prayer. In that moment, I realized I could keep living stubbornly trying to find satisfaction and fun in places that left me empty, or I could repent from all of that to what God had to offer. The next few years of high school I had left I spent with great godly friends, trying to reach my football team with this gospel that filled my life. Then, it was off to college.*

It wasn't too far into my college moments that my friends talked me into going to a house party—even before the first day of class. As soon as we walked in the door, it was as if I had walked onto the set of any college-based movie filled with beer pong, hooking up, and red Solo® cups. I remember it only took me forty-five minutes to decide not only to leave the party, but that that life had nothing valuable to offer me. The good news is that walking with Jesus doesn't really come along with a case of FOMO (fear of missing out). It's not as if there are only two options—choice A, the party, or B, sitting in your dorm and just going to class. There is a choice C, and it's Christ, along with all the joy and good times He has to offer inside godly community.

A month after that party, I met great friends like Taylor Lindley, who is still my best friend to this day. I actually had friends who cared about me as a person instead of pressuring me to become what they wanted me to be. My college experience was filled with road trips, camping trips, and house parties without alcohol, so I could actually remember the fun I had. I actually got to see how serving the church was life-giving and fun, not just a task. Small group Bible study became friends and me caring, challenging, and enjoying each other in life. My study abroad experience in Spain wasn't wasted getting wasted. It opened my eyes up to a whole new people and culture God loves while getting to surf pristine beaches, hike beautiful landscapes, try crazy-good food, learn Salsa dancing, and enjoy people from all over.

I had learned my lesson as a teenager. I'd rather listen to godly wisdom than have to be brought to repentance. I'm thankful God is a great, gracious Father who accepts me back after repenting and teaches me wisdom from my mistakes. But I'm much more thankful and much less scared when I humbly follow Jesus, maybe not knowing everything, but still reaping the joy of living faithfully with Him. Because I walked away from the party scene and walked in the wisdom God had given to me, I didn't miss out on anything in college. So choose the wisdom given by God rather than wisdom earned through mistakes.

—Zach Morris

Journal your thoughts and answers to the questions below and meet up with the person you've been walking with through this study to talk through some of your answers.

Practically speaking, what do you think wise living will look like over your next four(ish) years of your college experience?

What kinds of temptations do you foresee coming your way? What should you begin doing now to prepare for them?

Be honest: what role do you expect the local church to play during your college years?

What patterns do you need to establish now to help you in the months, years, and decades to come?

JOURNALING PAGES

LEADER GUIDE

LEADER TIPS

PRAYERFULLY PREPARE

Review. Review each session's material, Scripture, and questions ahead of time in order be best prepared for time with your group.

Pray. Be intentional about praying for each person in your group. Ask the Holy Spirit to work through you and the group discussion.

ENCOURAGE DISCUSSION

Everyone Is Included. Your goal is to foster a community in which everyone is welcomed just as they are but encouraged to grow spiritually.

Everyone Participates. Encourage everyone to answer and ask questions, share responses, and read aloud.

No One Dominates. Not even the leader. Politely redirect discussion if anyone dominates.

Nobody Is Rushed. Don't feel that a moment of silence is a bad thing. Students often need time to think about their responses to questions they've just heard or to gain courage to share what God is stirring in their hearts.

Input Is Affirmed. Make sure you point out something true or helpful in a response. Students are less likely to speak up if they fear that you don't actually want to hear their answers or that you're looking for only a certain answer.

God And His Word Are Central. Opinions and experiences can be helpful, but God has given us the truth.

KEEP CONNECTING

The more people are comfortable with and involved in one another's lives, the more they'll look forward to being together. When people move beyond being friendly to truly being friends who form a community, they come to each session eager to engage instead of just attending.

Encourage Community. Communicate with your group through the week with texts, social media, and even a school visit (if possible). But don't overdo it. Find the happy middle.

Encourage Deeper Relationships. Plan or spontaneously invite group members to join you outside your regularly scheduled group time for activities like a coffee or a meal, something fun like a ball game, or a service project.

SESSION 1: IDENTITY

GETTING STARTED

What is the most memorable trip you've ever taken? What was it about that trip that stood out to you?

STUDY

In your own words, what do you think the gospel is?

How have you seen the gospel affect your life?

Read **Genesis 1:1** and **Revelation 4:11**.

Why do you think we should start talking about the gospel by talking about God?

We were created in God's image, but as we move through what the gospel is, we learn that we veered away from Him.

Read **Jeremiah 17:9** and **Romans 3:23**.

What do you think the difference is between being a "good person" and being a sinner?

How can we say that "all have sinned"? What does it mean to be a sinner?

Read **2 Corinthians 5:20-21**.

Why is the resurrection of Jesus so crucial to the gospel?

How would you explain Jesus's sacrifice on the cross to someone who has never heard of it before?

What comes into your mind when you think about God?

Read each Scripture and describe what you learn about God through them: **Isaiah 6:1-8, Ephesians 2:1-10, Genesis 1, Job 38.**

What is the difference between the way the world sees us and the way God does?

How does that affect the way you go about your everyday life?

Read **Colossians 2:13-14**.

How does the gospel change the way you see yourself?

How does this new view of yourself motivate you to live?

SESSION 2: THE CHURCH

GETTING STARTED

Think about something cool that you're involved in right now. It might be an activity, a field you're studying, or an opportunity that has come your way. What are some of the things in your life that led you to this place?

STUDY

If you had to describe "church" in one or two sentences, what would you say?

Read **Acts 2:42-47**.

Look at some of the things the early church was involved in. What do you notice about it?

What do you think was attractive about the community described in this passage?

What about it would have made you want to join them?

Why do you think that the actions and attitudes of the people in the early church filled those around them with awe?

Think about your local church for a second. Where do you see these same actions and attitudes today?

Read **Hebrews 10:24-25**.

Consider what we read in Acts 2 along with this passage. Why is it so important for believers to meet together?

What do you miss out on by not being involved with a local body of believers?

Read **1 Corinthians 12:12-14**.

Why do you think a "body" is an appropriate metaphor for what the church is?

How does seeing the church as a "body" affect the way you see individual members of it?

Read **1 Peter 5:5**.

Why is it is important to respect and have relationships with older, more seasoned members of the body of Christ?

What is a way you've been grown in your process of sanctification by learning from generations who came before you?

SESSION 3: RELATIONSHIPS

GETTING STARTED

Who is the person you know best in the world? Describe them.

Who do you think knows you best? How do you know?

STUDY

Read **Luke 10:25-28**.

In your own words, what makes what is written in verse 27 the "greatest commandment"?

What kinds of actions show that you love the Lord?

What kinds of actions show that you love your neighbor as yourself?

Read **1 Corinthians 13:1-3**.

In your own words, what is love?

The Bible talks about four different kinds of love, each of which has its own word: *Agape, Philia, Eros, Storge.*

What do each of these kinds of love have in common?

How can you tell if someone is treating you with love?

Read **Matthew 5:43-48**.

What are some of the excuses we come up with to explain why someone in our lives isn't worth loving?

How have you seen people justify acting poorly to one another?

Have you ever been shown selfless love like the kind of love Jesus described in this passage?

How can the way you treat those around you communicate the gospel without even saying a word?

What are some ways that you see brokenness in the relationships around you?

How do Jesus's words in Matthew 5:43-48 address that brokenness?

SESSION 4: WISDOM

GETTING STARTED

When facing a new problem you've never faced before, which of these do you tend to do first?

Try to handle the problem yourself. If this is true for you, what has been the result when you've tried to handle a problem on your own?

Reach out to someone who knows how to do it better. If this is true for you, what has been the result when you've reached out to someone else to solve a problem?

STUDY

Read **James 1:5-8**.

In your own words, what do you think wisdom is?

How is it different than knowledge?

What places do people generally turn to when looking for wisdom?

Look back at James 1:5. What does it tell you about God's character?

How have you experienced God's generosity toward you?

Read **Proverbs 2:12-18**.

These words are thousands of years old, but still they feel fresh and relevant to us today. How do you see some of these situations still today?

Where do you think God's wisdom and the world's wisdom might contradict each other?

Read **Proverbs 3:5-12**.

Reflect on a time when you trusted someone, only to have that trust broken.

What does it take for you to put your trust in somebody?

What do you think it looks like to honor God with your possessions?

How would that affect the things that you want?

RETREAT GUIDE

HOW TO LEAD THIS STUDY IN A RETREAT SETTING.

An effective way of helping students engage with the content from *A Different College Experience* is in a retreat setting. A retreat gives students the opportunity to have space to process and wrestle with the material in a group setting and in an environment that is concentrated on this topic alone. Consider planning a weekend retreat to pour into high school seniors before they leave for college or for students who are already in college and let *A Different College Experience* be the material you use for teaching and group experiences.

Here are some ideas how you can integrate *A Different College Experience* in a retreat setting:

- Use Sessions 1-4, broken up over 2-3 days, as the content for group teaching and discussion. Encourage discussion and allow students to take the conversation deeper and more specific to their context during sessions.

- Build talks using the four session topics—Identity, the Church, Relationships, Wisdom—as the big picture ideas. Let the content from the session assist you in creating your outline.

- Use the questions from pages 66-67 as discussion guides for small group experiences.

- Ask students who have walked faithfully while in college to serve as group leaders or Q&A session panelists. Give opportunity for high schools students to ask questions to about how to successfully navigate the college experience and remain faithful to God in the process.

- Invite church staff to attend and share how students can plug in and serve in the local church while in college.

- Ask couples from your church who dated in college to share how they met and the role their faith played in their relationship.

- Bring in people who can help students know best practices for things like time management, study habits, money principles, and other things that are helpful to students in college.

Consider a schedule that looks like this:

Friday Night

Arrival	6:00pm
Dinner	6:30pm
Session 1: Identity	7:30pm
Small Group Discussion	8:30pm
Q&A: Staying Faithful in College	9:30pm

(Led by students who are living a different college experience)

Saturday Morning

Breakfast	8:00am
Session 2: The Church	9:00am
Small Group Discussion	10:00am
Q&A: How to Plug in and Serve	11:00am

(Led by church staff)

Saturday Afternoon

Lunch	12:00pm
Session 3: Relationships	1:00pm
Small Group Discussion	2:00pm
Q&A: How to date in college	3:00pm

(Led by married couples who successfully dated in college)

Saturday Evening

Dinner	6:00pm
Session 4: Wisdom	7:00pm
Small Group Discussion	8:00pm
Q&A: Best Practices	9:00pm

(Led by students and experts in different areas helpful for college students)

RESOURCES FOR LEADERS

LIfeway students has many other resources to help equip your students for college.

FOR LEADERS

The book this study is based on.

STUDENT MINISTRY THAT MATTERS

Student Ministry that Matters gives you and your leaders a framework to answer the question "Is my student ministry healthy?" and help you highlight areas of improvement as you seek to lead a student ministry focused on health.

WITHIN REACH

Research shows that the majority of teenagers who are active in church during high school stop attending shortly after. In a new study, Lifeway Student Ministry and Lifeway Research have partnered to identify the factors that are contributing to this disturbing trend as well as those factors that contribute to teens staying in church.

THE STUDENT MINISTRY PODCAST

The Lifeway Students blog and podcast are additional ways we want to come alongside you in the day-to-day realities of ministry. We hope they will be a hub of encouragement, experience, and practical advice for you as you strive to be obedient to God's call to make disciples of students and their families.

FOR STUDENTS

CHASING LOVE

Many people today think sex itself is the route to happiness. But Jesus showed that true happiness comes from loving God and loving others. In a culture filled with tension over sex, gender identity, same-sex relationships, pornography, and sexual abuse, we have to ask: Is it really possible to fully follow God's design for love and sexuality? Yes, it is.

EXPERIENCING GOD

When you open this book, you'll find that you aren't just reading; you are being remade, reoriented, and restored, captured not by a concept but by your Creator. Carefully listening to His voice will anchor you in His plan and set you free to live it with boldness and freedom.

DEFINED

You are a miracle. And that's exactly what this study is about—your true identity. Who you really are. The culture will try to define you, your past may try to label you, the enemy will seek to deceive you, but no one has the authority to give you your name—your identity—except your Father. And He says that your uniqueness is an expression of His creative genius and is designed to reflect His glory.

LIFEWAY STUDENTS DEVOTIONS

Thirty-day devotionals that address various topics, guiding students to a deeper walk and knowledge of God.

LEADER GUIDE 65

RESOURCES FOR COLLEGE STUDENTS

SOMEHOW YOU GOT THIS BOOK. YOU READ IT AND IT WAS REALLY HELPFUL. NOW WHAT?

Use the following questions for each session to serve as guides for discussion. You can use these in any setting, from coffee shops to dorm rooms to Zoom meetings. You can lead discussions yourself; you don't have to have a "leader." Having peer-led discussions is a great way to foster accountability and community in a group. You don't have to be perfect. You just have to love Jesus and desire to grow in your relationship with Him, resulting in Christlikeness being the goal you are aiming at with your life.

TIPS FOR LEADING DISCUSSION:

- Read the session.
- Meditate on the Scripture from the session.
- Review the discussion questions.
- Pray and ask God for wisdom, insight, and discernment.

SESSION 1: IDENTITY

What have been some of the ways you have identified yourself in the past? (We need pictures! We all want to see you when you were in your skater or cowboy phase.)

How does the gospel transcend the identities we might latch on to as "fads" or phases of our lives?

Where would you place yourself on the sanctification chart on page 16?

How would you explain the gospel to someone who had never heard of Jesus?

How would you explain the gospel to someone who grew up going to church but denied the claims of Jesus?

SESSION 2: THE CHURCH

Where have you found the greatest sense of community in your life? What made it such a great community?

When you read Acts 2 and compare it to the church today, where do you see similarities? Where do we fall short?

What role does the church play in your life right now?

The Bible describes the church as a body, dependent on each part to function correctly. What role do you play currently in the body?

How have you benefitted from a mentoring relationship with someone in the church?

SESSION 3: RELATIONSHIPS

Who was your best friend in second grade? Why were they your best friend? What did you do together that you enjoyed?

Jesus said the greatest commandment is to love God. How do we love God best at this stage in our lives as college students?

Jesus said the second greatest commandment is to love our neighbor as ourselves. How do we best love our neighbor as college students?

We see a lot of broken relationships around us at college. How can we foster healthy relationships, both in friendships and in dating relationships?

How can we in this group hold each other accountable with our relationships?

SESSION 4: WISDOM

Here's the scenario: the sink in your dorm room is stopped up and won't properly drain. What do you do?

What is the wisest counsel you've ever received? Why do you consider it to be such great wisdom?

When was a time you asked God for wisdom and He gave it to you? How difficult was it to do what you felt Him telling you to do?

What does it take for you to place your trust in someone else? What role does wisdom play in trusting others?

How can we help each other make wise choices?

RESOURCES FOR HIGH SCHOOL SENIORS

USE MASTER TEACHER OPTION WITH HIGH SCHOOL SENIORS.

Use this resource as a master teacher approach. Group students into tables with three to five students in them, led by an adult or even a student who has faithfully walked with God in college. Allow the master teacher to introduce the topic for the session and offer questions for discussion. The entire session should last approximately 60 minutes.

SESSION 1: IDENTITY

Icebreaker: What is the most memorable trip you've ever taken? What was it about that trip that stood out to you?

Master Teacher: Right now, you are on the verge of a great journey—college. In many ways, the Christian life is a journey, and the college years are a critical time for you in your Christian journey. The decisions you make during these years can accelerate you into a bright future or can set you back. The key to your journey as you approach college—and for the rest of your life—is the gospel.

Question: In your own words, what is the gospel?

Master Teacher: The gospel is not about us, it's about our Creator, His faithfulness, and His provision for us. He is perfect and holy. The gospel is His work in our lives, not something that we do to earn His favor. We were created in His image, but as we move through what the gospel is, we learn that it didn't take long before we veered away from Him.

Scripture: Read Romans 3:23.

> For all have sinned and fall short of the glory of God.

Question: Are people basically good or bad from the start? Defend your answer.

Master Teacher: Sin is how we have moved away from God, and unfortunately, our default setting is to be sinful from the time we are born (see Ps. 51:5). Our sinfulness is a problem we cannot fix on our own; we need someone to do for us what we cannot do for ourselves.

Scripture: Read 2 Corinthians 5:21.

> *He made the one who did not know sin to be sin for us, so that in him we might become the righteousness of God.*

Master Teacher: This verse is explaining what Jesus did to fix our sin problem. He lived a sinless life. He died on the cross, taking on our sin. He rose again from the grave three days later. He did all the things we cannot.

Question: How would you explain to someone else what Jesus did on the cross?

Master Teacher: The key really is Jesus rising from the grave. If Jesus didn't rise from the dead, He wasn't who He said He was, and the penalty we owe for our sin hasn't been paid. Fortunately for us, Jesus is who He said He is. He did rise from the dead. He did conquer sin and death on the cross. He rose from the grave, doing exactly what He said He would do, proving Himself to be the only Savior we can put our faith in.

Question: How does this explanation of Jesus's death and resurrection impact the way you see God?

Master Teacher: God is not a piece of the puzzle; He is the entire frame. He is the lens through which you see everything and everyone. He is the one who makes the other pieces fit. Seeing God for who He is doesn't only change the way we see God, it changes the way we view ourselves.

Scripture: Read Colossians 2:13-14.

> *And when you were dead in trespasses and in the uncircumcision of your flesh, he made you alive with him and forgave us all our trespasses. He erased the certificate of debt, with its obligations, that was against us and opposed to us, and has taken it away by nailing it to the cross.*

Question: How does the gospel change the way you see yourself? How does this view of yourself motivate you to live?

Master Teacher: If you are a child of God, you are forgiven. You have been made clean. Whenever God looks at you, He doesn't see the one who was dead, He sees someone who has been made clean by Jesus's sacrifice. Your sin has been nailed to the cross, and He has removed the guilt and shame that goes along with it. This reality is not just an interesting fact about us; it's everything about who we are. It's our identity. This truth guides us, and it's crucial to us getting the college experience right.

Discussion Questions: What are some steps you can take to further embrace the gospel as the central truth of your life and identity?

What elements of the gospel—forgiveness, removal of guilt and shame, God's perception of you, etc.—do you struggle to embrace as your identity?

What are practical steps you can take to make the gospel the focus of your college experience?

Close in prayer.

SESSION 2: THE CHURCH

Icebreaker: Think about something you are involved in currently. It could be a sport or instrument you play, an activity or hobby you do in your spare time, or even a group or club that you belong to. How did you get involved with this? What led you to become interested in it?

Master Teacher: We don't usually think about it this way, but one of the oldest movements that people still take part in is Jesus's church. Let's take a few minutes to talk about what the church is and why it's so incredible and important to take part in to make the most of your college experience.

Question: If someone asked you to describe the church, what would you say?

Master Teacher: For all practical purposes, the church is just a bunch of people who are all devoted to the same idea: that Jesus is the Son of God, that He is risen, and that these truths motivate us to live in a certain way.

Scripture: Read Acts 2:42-47.

> *They devoted themselves to the apostles' teaching, to the fellowship, to the breaking of bread, and to prayer.*
>
> *Everyone was filled with awe, and many wonders and signs were being performed through the apostles. Now all the believers were together and held all things in common. They sold their possessions and property and distributed the proceeds to all, as any had need. Every day they devoted themselves to meeting together in the temple, and broke bread from house to house. They ate their food with joyful and sincere hearts, praising God and enjoying the favor of all the people. Every day the Lord added to their number those who were being saved.*

Question: What was attractive about the early church to you?

Master Teacher: The amazing thing about the church at this point was that it was wildly unstructured, yet it perfectly fit the needs of the people it reached. They didn't even have their own building!

Question: Where do you see the same actions and attitudes in the church today?

Master Teacher: The Greek word used for "community" in this passage is koinonia. When people share koinonia, it means something different than just being in close proximity to each other. It means that they are united by a common goal—in this case, the gospel of Jesus. Because of what united them, it didn't matter what they looked like or where they came from. They had the most powerful unifying factor right at their center—the gospel.

Scripture: Read Hebrews 10:24-25.

> *And let us consider one another in order to provoke love and good works, not neglecting to gather together, as some are in the habit of doing, but encouraging each other, and all the more as you see the day approaching.*

Question: What do you miss out on when you're not involved with a local body of believers?

Master Teacher: Whenever we see the church mentioned in Scripture, it actually goes a lot deeper than just acknowledging it as a group of people united with a common goal. It serves a function much bigger than that: it is called the body of Christ. Since Jesus is not physically present among us, we are called His body. When the world wants to see what Jesus looks like, they should look no further than the church.

Scripture: Read 1 Corinthians 12:12-14.

> *For just as the body is one and has many parts, and all the parts of that body, though many, are one body—so also is Christ. For we were all baptized by one Spirit into one body—whether Jews or Greeks, whether slaves or free—and we were all given one Spirit to drink. Indeed, the body is not one part but many.*

Question: Why is the body an appropriate metaphor for what the church is intended to be?

Master Teacher: Since the church is the physical representation of Christ to the world, that means each member has incredible individual worth. When a body is perfectly functioning, each of its organs, systems, and limbs are working together with the rest of the body to achieve the overall goal of health and productivity. The church is not going to be full of productive members if the members are isolated and operating all on their own accord. We must learn to work together in humility if we're going to be the healthy body of Christ.

Scripture: Read 1 Peter 5:5.

> *In the same way, you who are younger, be subject to the elders. All of you clothe yourselves with humility toward one another, because God resists the proud but gives grace to the humble.*

Question: Why is important to have relationships with and learn from more seasoned members of the body of Christ?

Master Teacher: One of the simplest ways to ensure you are working as a productive member of Christ's body is to learn from those who've been where you are before. Being plugged into a local, healthy body of Christ is absolutely essential for anybody living out their faith in Jesus and pursuing sanctification.

Discussion Questions: How does seeing the church as a "body" affect the way you see individual members of it?

What is a way you've been grown in your process of sanctification by learning from generations who came before you?

What are some steps you can take to ensure that being involved in the local church becomes a vital part of your college experience?

Close in Prayer.

SESSION 3: RELATIONSHIPS

Icebreaker: Who is the person you know best in the world? How did you get to know them so well?

Master Teacher: One of the purest joys we can experience in life is that of being known. When we can be ourselves around someone else and know that we can trust them, and that they can trust us, we experience the kind of beauty that comes from true, authentic relationships. As Christians, we're called to a high standard when it comes to those around us. God has made the standard for treating others unmistakably clear. As we learn to treat them the way we've been commanded to, we'll learn about ourselves, other people, and God.

Scripture: Read Luke 10:25-28.

> Then an expert in the law stood up to test him, saying, "Teacher, what must I do to inherit eternal life?"
>
> "What is written in the law?" he asked him. "How do you read it?"
>
> He answered, "Love the Lord your God with all your heart, with all your soul, with all your strength, and with all your mind," and "your neighbor as yourself."
>
> "You've answered correctly," he told him. "Do this and you will live."

Master Teacher: This commandment is actually two separate ones, but they flow together perfectly: if you love God with everything that you are, that love will naturally flow out to the people around you. The reason is simple: if we love God, we will love those who bear God's image the same way. Every person ever created, no matter who they are, was created by God with the incredibly important distinction of being made in His image (see Gen. 1:26-27). We cannot claim to love God if we do not love the people around us.

Question: What kinds of actions show that you love the Lord? What kinds of actions show that you love your neighbor as yourself?

Scripture: Read 1 Corinthians 13:1-3.

> If I speak human or angelic tongues but do not have love, I am a noisy gong or a clanging cymbal. If I have the gift of prophecy and understand all mysteries and all knowledge, and if I have all faith so that I can move mountains but do not have love, I am nothing. And if I give away all my possessions, and if I give over my body in order to boast but do not have love, I gain nothing.

Master Teacher: The ancient Greeks used four different words for love, each of which has its own meaning: Agape means unconditional love, like God's love for us. Philia refers to brotherly love, like the love between friends. Eros means romantic love, like the love between spouses. Storge is familial love, like the love from a parent to a child or between siblings. Each of these loves refers to a different person that love is directed toward. However, the verses in 1 Corinthians we just read speaks to them all.

Question: How can you tell if someone is treating you with love?

Master Teacher: Not everyone is going to be able to communicate with you in the specific way that you receive love best. But you can always tell if someone is treating you with love if they are showing you selflessness and respect. This is how Paul can say that it doesn't matter what good we accomplish or what feats we can manage if we aren't motivated by love. If we can't show our neighbor love—no matter who they are—how can we say that we love the Creator who made them?

Scripture: Read Matthew 5:43-48.

> "You have heard that it was said, Love your neighbor and hate your enemy. But I tell you, love your enemies and pray for those who persecute you, so that you may be children of your Father in heaven. For he causes his sun to rise on the evil and the good, and sends rain on the righteous and the unrighteous. For if you love those who love you, what reward will you have? Don't even the tax collectors do the same? And if you greet only your brothers and sisters, what are you doing out of the ordinary? Don't even the Gentiles do the same? Be perfect, therefore, as your heavenly Father is perfect."

Master Teacher: In this passage, Jesus laid out the standard for how we are to treat even our greatest enemies. These can be difficult words to read because it is not easy to love other people, especially if they've wronged us. But Jesus made no distinctions or exceptions.

Question: How can the way you treat those around you communicate the gospel without even saying a word?

Master Teacher: You are going into some of the most crucial years of your lives. You will be surrounded by people you weren't around growing up, who believe all sorts of things about the way that people are supposed to treat each other. That is okay. Jesus has called us to live in this tension. The kind of love we are to show those around us is not something that has an earthly origin: it comes from God, who loved us first in the same way.

College is a wonderful time for relationships, but it can also be destructive. Keeping this foundational view of love at the forefront of your mind and heart and applying it to all your relationships can keep you from decisions that can negatively alter your life and can help fortify friendships that will last a lifetime.

Discussion Questions: What steps can you take to let God's view of relationships, described in the Scripture passages we read today, be your guide as you build relationships in college?

How have you seen friendships build people up? How have friendships torn people down? How do you live like the type of friend that builds up?

How can you apply each of these three Scripture passages to dating relationships while you are in college?

Close in prayer.

SESSION 4: WISDOM

Icebreaker: When facing a new problem you've never encountered before, which of these do you tend to do first?

A) Try to handle the problem yourself. If so, what has been the result when you've tried to handle a problem on your own?

B) Reach out to someone who knows how to do it better. If so, what has been the result when you've reached out to someone else to solve a problem?

Master Teacher: Whether you try to fix it yourself or get help, eventually, you're going to come across situations that aren't solved simply. You'll need wisdom. Wisdom can be quite a bit trickier than we tend to give it credit for. During your college years, very little will be more useful for your experience than finding wisdom.

Scripture: Read James 1:5-8.

> Now if any of you lacks wisdom, he should ask God—who gives to all generously and ungrudgingly—and it will be given to him. But let him ask in faith without doubting. For the doubter is like the surging sea, driven and tossed by the wind. That person should not expect to receive anything from the Lord, being double-minded and unstable in all his ways.

Question: In your own words, what do you think wisdom is? How is it different than knowledge?

Master Teacher: Wisdom is the ability to decide right from wrong, whether that means discerning the right attitude to have or the right action to take. There are many places we turn to when looking for wisdom, ranging from trusted mentors, social media, and even sometimes simply "trusting our gut." James said that we should go first to the One who gives wisdom to any who ask before we go to other sources.

Question: Have you ever asked God for wisdom? What was the result when you did?

Master Teacher: The more we experience God, the more we find that generosity is one of His most apparent qualities and His mercy is unending. He is our Shepherd, and His wisdom is one of the tools He generously gives to safeguard us from walking into something that could cause us harm. Going into this season of your life, you will be facing new situations and decisions you have not experienced before, and you will need wise decision-making.

Scripture: Read Proverbs 2:12-15.

> [Wisdom] will rescue you from the way of evil—from anyone who says perverse things, from those who abandon the right paths to walk in ways of darkness, from those who enjoy doing evil and celebrate perversion, whose paths are crooked, and whose ways are devious.

Question: These words are thousands of years old, but still they feel fresh and relevant to us today. How do you see some of these situations still today?

Master Teacher: People haven't fundamentally changed over the years. We still struggle with the same things, there are just new ways to do the same old things today. If you go into college relying on worldly wisdom, odds are you are going to end up pretty frustrated. You can find any number of worldly philosophies to justify any actions you could ever take. But these next few years could be an incredible opportunity to do something that will set a foundation under your feet for years to come: to grow in godly wisdom.

Scripture: Read Proverbs 3:5-8.

> *Trust in the Lord with all your heart, and do not rely on your own understanding; in all your ways know him, and he will make your paths straight. Don't be wise in your own eyes; fear the Lord and turn away from evil. This will be healing for your body and strengthening for your bones.*

Question: When have you trusted someone, only to have that trust broken?

Master Teacher: The unfortunate truth is that each of you probably has a story about putting your trust in somebody else and being let down by them. This is not to say we shouldn't learn to trust the people around us; rather, it should highlight how exceptional it is to trust the Lord. And what is most remarkable about all of this is that as you put more and more trust in Him, He will never let you down. The college experience is just plain better when it's not littered with bad decision after bad decision. The way to avoid bad decisions is to lean on the wisdom that comes from God.

Discussion Questions: What are some real-life scenarios where you'll need wisdom in college? What will be step one in discerning the right thing to do in these situations?

What do you do when you've made a bad choice? How do you overcome it and keep moving forward with your life and relationship with God?

How can we be people who encourage others to make wise choices and give wise counsel as well as offer grace when our friends have made poor choices?

Close in prayer.

NOTES

SOURCES

1. Wayne Grudem, Bible Doctrine (Grand Rapids, MI: 1999), 329.

2. Nathan Bingham, "What Is Sanctification," Ligonier Ministries, June 24, 2013; https://www.ligonier.org/blog/what-sanctification/

3. "Elon Musk." Biography.com. A&E Networks Television, April 7, 2021. https://www.biography.com/business-figure/elon-musk.

Excerpts included in the Personal Study on pages 15-16, 27-28, 39-40, and 51-52 are taken from A Different College Experience by Ben Trueblood and Brian Mills (B&H Publishing Group, 2019).

You can have a different college experience.

By letting the gospel inform four major categories—identity, the church, relationships, and wisdom—this Bible study reveals to students how to have a different, but fulfilling, college experience.

Written from a pastor's heart, Ben Trueblood and Brian Mills, lay out how to avoid the major pitfalls and obstacles that derail so many students during their college years. College can be some of the best years of a person's life, and this study shows how to make them enjoyable and productive instead of being filled with mistakes and regret.

The Bible study includes four sessions with discussion guides and many other resources that can equip students and leaders in preparation for the college experience.

- Explore how the gospel shapes our identity.
- See the major role the church plays in our lives.
- Learn how to see others and honor God in relationships.
- Gain wisdom for the journey.

ADDITIONAL RESOURCES

A Different College Experience
A guide to following Christ in college, written from the heart of a pastor. From B&H Books.

A Different College Experience (e-book)
A 4-week study preparing and equipping students for the college experience.